BASEBALL

By Mark Littleton

ZondervanPublishingHouse
Grand Rapids, Michigan

A Division of HarperCollins*Publishers*

Baseball

Copyright © 1995 by Mark Littleton

Requests for information should be addressed to:
Zondervan Publishing House
Grand Rapids, Michigan 49530

Library of Congress Cataloging-in-Publication Data

Littleton, Mark R., 1950–
    Baseball / Mark Littleton.
       p. cm.—(Sports heroes)
    Includes bibliographical references.
    ISBN: 0–310–49551-2 (softcover)
     1. Baseball players—United States—Biography—Juvenile lit-
erature. 2. Baseball players—United States—Religious life—
Juvenile literature. I. Title. II. Series: Littleton, Mark R., 1950–
Sports heroes.
  GV884.A1L58   1995
  796.357'092'2–dc20   94–44930
  [B]   CIP
                                            AC

Edited by Tom Raabe
Interior design by Joe Vriend

Printed in the United States of America

    96 97 98 99 00 / ❖ DC / 10 9 8 7 6 5 4 3

*To the Little League of Langston Field
and the local Barclay League,
Cherry Hill, New Jersey, 1958–62.
I wasn't that good,
but I learned the game
and continue to love it.*

Contents

Let's Hear it for Sports Heroes

Sports heroes are a special kind of hero. They don't have a once-in-a-lifetime experience where they perform stupendously. They're not the guy who jumps in the river and pulls out the drowning girl just before she goes under for the last time. Those kinds of stories make headlines, and the hero behind them enjoys maybe a day or a week in the sunlight of fame.

Sports heroes, though, have a different opportunity. They can perform heroically day after day, season after season. Every game is a new chance to inspire their fans. Every time at bat is a moment in the sun. Every ball hit to their area of the field is an opportunity for an amazing feat. They go out on the diamond and become heroes every day for years.

And yet, there are other moments. Those moments when everything they have and are is on the line. That split second when a wrong move can mean destruction, and a right move can mean destiny.

Every one of the men in this book has had such moments. That one crack at fame. That one story that has inspired millions.

I hope you will read with that truth in mind. I've tried to select moments when each of these heroes excelled in some special, perhaps eternal, way. They are true heroes, men raised up by God for a time such as ours. Read of them and thank our Lord that he made them what they are: people whom we can follow and love and imitate to the best of our abilities.

Mark Littleton
February, 1995

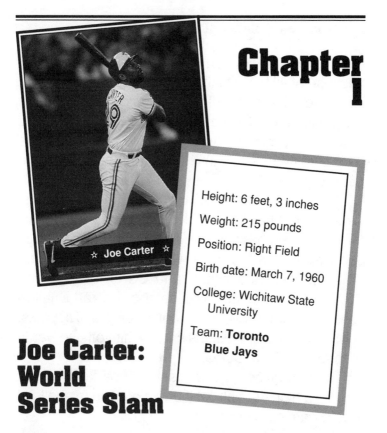

Chapter 1

Height: 6 feet, 3 inches

Weight: 215 pounds

Position: Right Field

Birth date: March 7, 1960

College: Wichitaw State University

Team: **Toronto Blue Jays**

★ Joe Carter ★

Joe Carter: World Series Slam

The World Series, 1993. Game Six. The Toronto Blue Jays are ahead of the Philadelphia Phillies, three games to two. It's the bottom of the ninth inning. The score is 6–5, Phillies leading. Mitch Williams, the Phillies' ace closer, is pitching. If he can get the Blue Jays out, it will force another game, a seventh game. And anything can happen in a seventh game.

Williams had seen such situations many times

before. In fact, he won his nickname "Wild Thing" because of all the wild things he did in closing. Often, he would get himself into trouble and have everyone screaming for his head. Then he'd work his way out of it, almost miraculously. He could be wild, but he had saved 43 games in 51 appearances during the past year.

And now, in Game Six of the 1993 World Series, he is in trouble again. Rickey Henderson and Paul Molitor are on base for the Blue Jays, with one out. Joe Carter is at the plate with a 2–1 count on him. Williams throws a slider, and Carter swings and misses. Count, 2–2. Phillie catcher Darren Daulton calls for another slider. The philosophy is: if it works, keep using it. But Williams shakes him off. He wants to throw heat—a fastball.

Daulton gives in. Okay, serve up a fastball. But let it be a high fastball, let it be an outside fastball, let it be a hard-to-hit fastball.

It isn't. It's down and in.

Carter likes such pitches, even though he often hooks them foul. Still, he swings.

Wham! The ball is in the air. Carter loses it in the lights. He's on his way to first.

He sees the ball again as he reaches first. It's over the fence and straight into the Blue Jays' bull pen—379 feet from home plate. Home run! Three runs score. The Blue Jays win, 8–6. The Series is over, and the Blue Jays have taken the title for the second year in a row.

As for Joe Carter, he had fulfilled every kid and baseball lover's ultimate dream: he had hit a home run in the ninth inning of the last game of the World Series while his team was behind *to win the game*. A shot for eternity. Suddenly, Joe Carter was a hero like he'd never been. One other player, Pittsburgh Pirate Bill Mazeroski, in 1960, hit a ninth-inning home run to win the final game of a World Series, but he hit his when the score was tied. No one had ever done it with his team playing catch-up in a World Series.

This wasn't the first time Carter had hit a game-winning home run in the ninth in his major-league life. The first was in 1986 against Dan Quisenberry of the Kansas City Royals. But while that was just an ordinary, forgotten game, this one in the World Series made history.

So, who is this man who slammed a 379-foot homer into the Blue Jays' bull pen to become a hero?

Joe Carter grew up

13

in a churchgoing family in Oklahoma City. For him, though, church was something his parents made him do. He lived for sports: football, basketball, and baseball. He was so good that as a fifteen-year-old sophomore he led his high school football team to a state championship. That same year, the basketball team also won the state championship. He should have been as elated as he could be.

But he wasn't. There was an emptiness inside. He actually felt a little disappointed. Was this all there was in life? If it was, life wasn't all it was cracked up to be.

The next year neither team won a championship, but in his senior year his basketball team did. Joe even scored eleven points in the last two minutes of the game. He was leaving high school in style, even if he still felt a little empty.

Joe went on to Wichita State University on a baseball scholarship. He decided to play only two sports there: baseball and football. It was at Wichita that Joe met someone who changed his life—his roommate, Kevin Scott. Kevin was a committed kind of guy who talked nothing but football. Then, in his sophomore year, Kevin was injured in the back. He was told that if he ever got a hit like that in the back again, he'd be paralyzed for life. Kevin gave up football. But his zest for life and commitment didn't waver, and he got involved in church. Suddenly, this

14

kid who talked nothing but football was talking nothing but Jesus Christ.

Joe didn't know how to take it. Soon, he was doing all he could to avoid Kevin. Yet he couldn't avoid what he saw in Kevin's life: peace, happiness, enthusiasm, a joy that he himself admired. Finally, one day Joe gave up. He became a Christian. He says, "It was the first time in my life I made the decision to trust Jesus Christ. Now that I was away from home, I could make the decision on my own and not because somebody else made me do it. For the first time in my life I felt in my heart exactly that love and peace that Kevin Scott was talking about. It gave me a whole different perspective on people and on life."[1]

But becoming a Christian didn't diminish Joe's desire to play and compete. If anything, it made him realize how great his responsibility was. "One thing I like to do is lead by example. Some people take Christianity and say, 'Ah, just another religion.' But the real question they want to know is, 'Are you living it?' A lot of people don't want to hear what you have to say—they want to see it in your life."[2]

He describes his walk with the Lord this way:

My relationship to Christ is what's important to me now. He's made some great changes in my heart. I never drank or smoked or got into drugs. That I didn't have to give up those things made my conversion a little easier on my flesh. But God really dealt with my heart attitudes. God developed a quiet spirit within me and I saw people in a totally different way.

Not long after I was saved, one of the baseball coaches at Wichita jumped all over me for something. Before Christ came in, I would have jumped all over him. I really thought I could do no wrong. I had survived growing up in a family of eleven. I helped out at my dad's gas station and even drove cars around at the age of eight. I was mature. But here I learned what real maturity was all about. I didn't talk back to my coach. I accepted what he said and went to work on the problem.[3]

That attitude imbues everything Joe does today.

In 1981, Joe was *The Sporting News*'s College Player of the Year coming out of Wichita State. He was a first-round draft pick of the Chicago Cubs. He has played for the Cubs, Indians, Padres, and now the Blue Jays.

Joe has hit three home runs in a single game four times during his career. He's been an all-star twice and has knocked in more than 100 runs in four consecutive seasons. His 119 RBI (runs batted in) in 1992 for the Blue Jays was the second highest in the American League that year. He's had a lot of honors. But being part of the Blue Jays has been the triumph and climax of his career.

The 1993 World Series was a battle all the way. Toronto took the first two games, then lost the third on the Phillies' home turf. Then they split the next two with the Phillies before Joe's big hit won the final game.

The fourth game of that series was remarkable in many ways. Thirteen records were broken or tied in the game. It was the longest World Series game in history, going four hours and fourteen minutes. It was also the highest-scoring.

Joe Carter was relentless in the fourth game. He hit a single and scored one of the Jays' three runs in the first inning. The Phillies came back with four to make the score 4–3, Phillies. There were an astonishing six walks in that first inning, played in a cold drizzle. In the second inning, Toronto was held scoreless, but Philadelphia added two more runs to make it 6–3.

In the fifth inning, Blue Jays' reliever Al Leiter came to bat for the first time in his major-league career. He promptly sent the ball into left field for a double. 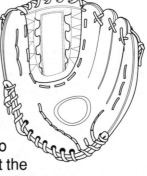 They weren't even expecting him to hit! However, the Phils added another five runs to their total, making it 12–7 by the end of the inning.

At that point, the Blue Jays called for Tony Castillo to come in from the bull pen. But the phones weren't working properly, and

Mark Eichhorn mistakenly walked out to the mound. Cito Gaston, the Blue Jays' manager, rushed out and soon 23 people gathered around the mound trying to make sense of what was going on. Eventually they gave Gaston a walkie-talkie (which didn't work) to talk to the bull pen. In the end, he had to send runners back and forth.

In the sixth inning, Phillies' manager Jim Fregosi called in David West to relieve. His ERA (earned run average) at that point in the World Series was the worst ever: infinity. He hadn't gotten a single batter out—eight batters had faced him, and all eight got on base! West hurled that inning. The first two batters he was up against hit, but then West made Joe Carter fly out to right field, and his ERA came down to 162.00. The Jays scored two in the sixth and the Phils came back with one.

Going into the seventh inning, the Blue Jays sent Tony Castillo, their pitcher, to the plate. Normally, a pinch hitter would have batted for Castillo in such a situation, but there was no hitter left to replace him. The Jays were mowed down that inning, and the Phils added one more run to their total, making it 14–9.

Then came the top of the eighth. Carter was up second with one out. He singled. Then a base on balls and an error. Then the Blue Jays went on a hitting streak that scored six runs. The team batted around, starting and ending with Alomar, who grounded out each time to third base.

The score was now 15–14, and the Phillies didn't come back. His next at bat, Joe hit a double, but it didn't matter. The Blue Jays had just won the longest, highest-scoring game in World Series history. Fourteen relievers were used in the game, six by the Blue Jays and eight by the Phillies. One of the fans held up a sign, "WILL PITCH MIDDLE RELIEF FOR FOOD," echoing the signs homeless people use to raise money begging in the city.

The next day, the Phillies received phone calls threatening the life of Mitch Williams, the pitcher in that terrible eighth inning of Game Four. But that night, Curt Schilling pitched a shutout for the Phils to put the Series at 3–2, Blue Jays, and it looked like the Phillies' uphill struggle was gathering steam.

How can the Jays score fifteen runs in one game and none in the next? One reason: that's baseball. Joe Carter says, "Let's say I hit three home runs in the last three games, and I'm looking good. Well, I get up to bat in the next game and I go hitless. Baseball has a way of humbling you."[4]

Then came that dramatic sixth game. Dave Stewart pitched a four-hitter for the Blue Jays for the first six innings to build up a 5–1 lead. But the Phillies caught fire in the seventh, cranking out five runs, three on a home run by Lenny Dykstra. Things looked good for the Phillies. The Phils let the Blue

Jays load the bases in the eighth, but held them scoreless. Three men left on, no runs.

Finally, they reached the bottom of the ninth. Mitch "Wild Thing" Williams was closing again. The first batter walked, the second flew out to left, and the third singled. Then Joe Carter stepped to the plate and drilled the three-run home run that won the 1993 World Series.

What does Joe say about it all? "Don't be afraid to live out your dreams. Don't be afraid of failure, either. If you fail, so what? If I was out in the ninth inning, there was another guy coming up behind me."[5]

But he wasn't out.

He was hero for a day.

And perhaps for a century!

---

1. Dave Branon and Joe Pellegrino, *Safe at Home* (Chicago: Moody, 1992), 90–91.

2. Branon and Pellegrino, 91.

3. Bill Alexson, *Batting a Thousand* (Nashville: Nelson, 1990), 50–51.

4. Alexson, 91.

5. Steve Rushin, "Home Sweet Home," *Sports Illustrated,* 1 November 1993, 2.

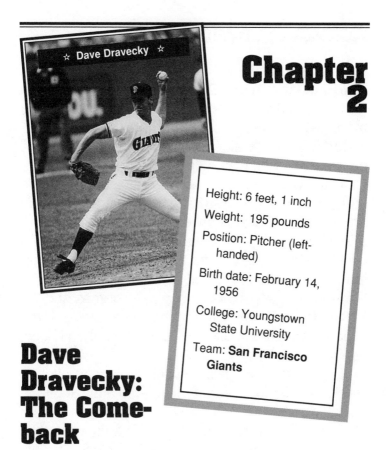

☆ Dave Dravecky ☆

Chapter 2

Height: 6 feet, 1 inch

Weight: 195 pounds

Position: Pitcher (left-handed)

Birth date: February 14, 1956

College: Youngstown State University

Team: **San Francisco Giants**

Dave Dravecky: The Come-back

For most of us, August 10, 1989, was just another day. For Dave Dravecky, a pitcher for the San Francisco Giants, it is a day that will live in his memory as his greatest baseball triumph. That day he returned to the major leagues after living through a pitcher's nightmare: cancer in the largest muscle of his left arm. His pitching arm.

The cancer started in 1987 as a little lump in his deltoid muscle, when Dave was in his sixth season with the San Diego Padres. At first he thought it was a muscle spasm or perhaps a knot. When he consulted with his trainer about it, he reached the conclusion that it was nothing to worry about.

Dave was traded to the Giants and started with that team on July 4, 1987. Prior to the trade, Dave's arm spent a lot of time on ice and under the trainer's eye with massages and jacuzzi water therapy. The Giants were in a pennant battle with several other teams, and Dave wanted to contribute. With the Padres, he'd pitched relief in playoff games and the 1984 World Series, running up ten and two-thirds scoreless innings. With the Giants, he hoped to do it again.

Dave Dravecky calls himself a pinpoint pitcher. He does not "blow batters away" with a blazing fastball as do Roger Clemens, Nolan Ryan, and Dwight Gooden. Rather, he pitches to a batter's weakness and fools him with pitches aimed at precise points around the plate. He strikes people out with feints, tricks, and little heists. Like Orel Hershiser, he's the thinking man's pitcher. The way Dave himself says you can tell if he's "on" is by counting how many bats he breaks in the course of a game. Typically, Dave will throw what is called a "backdoor slider." Since he's left-handed, to a right-handed hitter that brand of slider comes in on the outside, then breaks in and down right over the outside corner of the plate. After seeing the slider, a batter tends to lean in on the next pitch.

So what does Dravecky throw then? An inside fastball. It catches the batter leaning too much and he swings wildly, striking the ball on the handle of the bat, which will frequently break in the process.

During the National League playoff game against the St. Louis Cardinals, Dave destroyed five bats. All broken on that inside fastball.

Dave Dravecky was pitching the game of his life. A crowd of 55,331 watched as Dravecky threw sliders, curves, and a fastball that reached 88 miles per hour, breaking bats and perhaps a few hearts. The fans were not with Dravecky, though. They wanted him to lose. This was Cardinal turf.

Each inning, the stadium grew quiet as Dravecky stood, wound up, and threw. The best hitters in the league struck out, popped out, grounded out, flew out. At the end of the fourth inning it was 3–0, Giants. Busch Stadium was silent and intent as a cat poised to strike. Dravecky had to go down. The Cardinals weren't giving up this game!

Dravecky's heart, though, surged with confidence. He was on. And on. And on. His pinpoint precision put everything right where he wanted it. And not a Cardinal drew blood. At the end, he had given up only two hits and no runs. Nearly a perfect game. A shutout in the playoffs!

Added to his other playoff and World Series pitching stints, Dravecky had recorded nineteen and two-thirds scoreless innings. The Giants won the game, 5–0. Afterwards, to reporters and on the news, Dravecky gave a testimony of his faith in Christ. And the *San Francisco Chronicle* would write of his flawless pitching, "It was so easy it seemed effortless. It was so effortless it seemed boring."

But not to Dave Dravecky. This had been the game of his life.

Or was it?

No, several more games lay ahead that would change his life—and baseball history.

That winter, the little lump in his arm kept getting bigger. In January 1988, he underwent a CAT scan and an MRI (magnetic resonance image) at the Scripps Clinic by the Giants' orthopedic (bone and muscle) team. There were no precise results. The doctors told Dave to watch the lump and come back in six months.

Spring training 1988 was "baseball heaven" for Dave. For rookies, spring training is a time of agony and worry. But for veterans, it's a relaxing, fun time. For Dave and his family, it was also a time of renewal, Bible study, long conversations into the night, and plain fun and fellowship with Christian friends on the team. In fact, there were so many vocal Christians on the Giants that they came to be known as the "God Squad." And that was not a term of respect!

Dave went into the season with high hopes. His first game out that year against the Dodgers was close to a shutout—the Giants won it, 5–1. It looked like Dave's year. He was going to have a 20-win season, or better!

Things didn't proceed that way, though. Despite that start, an increasingly sore shoulder bothered Dave constantly. His second game was a loss, followed by two no-decisions in which he pitched poorly and lasted only a few innings. His fifth time out, he pitched well for eight innings and collected a second win. Then, in his sixth game, the Cardinals, perhaps remembering the shutout in the National League Championship Series the year before, whammed and slammed Dravecky's pitches all over the field. Another loss racked up.

Meanwhile, real disaster struck: The Giants placed Dave on the fifteen-day disabled list. The management decided that his sore arm needed a rest.

Back with the team on May 28,

Dave pitched terribly against the Phillies despite his long rest. Two days later in Montreal, he couldn't even throw the ball in the bull pen. The pitching coach, Norm Sherry, sent Dave in for medical testing.

Tests and medical observation led to nothing. The pain continued. Even when he was sent to the minors for a 20-day stretch, Dave couldn't pitch. Something was terribly wrong, and no one seemed to know what it was.

That fall, Dave underwent more testing in his hometown of Youngstown, Ohio. During that time Dave was informed by his doctor, "It's a tumor." An oncologist, a tumor specialist, soon determined that the tumor, probably benign, was located in the deltoid muscle of Dave's upper left arm. Dr. Mark Roh, a relative of Dave's wife, Janice, called to explain it all to Janice. "It's the best it could be for what it is," he said. "If Dave had to get cancer, this is the kind you would want it to be. There are many different kinds of cancer. This is the best kind of cancer to have."[1]

The growth was called a desmoid tumor. They're "good," in that they're unlikely to spread through the body and become lethal. Thus, caught early, such tumors can be surgically removed. Frequently, there is no recurrence of the cancer.

The problem for Dave Dravecky, though, was that this tumor had fixed itself to the main bone in his upper arm, the humerus. It was also firmly embedded in the deltoid muscle of his arm and shoulder. The deltoid is the main muscle in the upper arm, the one that enables a pitcher to throw a ball hard, fast, with various spins, and most of all, with control. If bone and muscle were removed along with the tumor, it could mean the end of Dave's baseball career.

It wasn't an easy decision, but in the end, Dave didn't hesitate. Losing his life and everything in it in order to preserve a baseball career was foolhardy. He told his surgeon, Dr. George Muschler, to plan for an operation.

Dave's faith in Christ strengthened him. He and his wife prayed repeatedly throughout that time. When Dr. Muschler told him again it might mean the end of his baseball career, Dave said, "Don't think I'm going to go off in a little closet and cry. I've had a great career, I've enjoyed every minute of it, and I'm ready to go on with whatever is next."[2]

It was an admirable, perhaps astonishing attitude. But in the days ahead, Dave would find it was an attitude he'd have to struggle to maintain.

On October 7, 1988, Dr. Muschler removed the tumor along with half of Dave's deltoid muscle. Part of his humerus was also frozen. This meant that for at least six months to a year he could be in danger of breaking his arm if he tried to pitch again.

It was a tough recovery period, but after two months Dave began to think about a comeback. Was it possible?

He underwent a number of tests and adjustments. No one thought he could ever pitch again, especially on a major-league level. But as Dave worked out after Christmas, he felt stronger and better. On January 9, 1989, he stood before a panel of doctors showing them what he could do. His ability to reach and bend with that left arm amazed them all. Nearly everyone proclaimed it a miracle.

In the end, the doctors gave him permission to get into a rehabilitation program with his team trainer. For the next few months, Dave worked out with weights and a stationary bicycle and threw a football. His arm began to limber up, and he even started throwing a baseball.

Many thought it was still impossible. Dave, his wife, and several teammates who shared his faith in Christ prayed together over the next months, asking God to give Dave the right attitude about a comeback, whether it was possible or not. Larry Brown, who had a clinic in Palo Alto, California, helped Dave get back to full strength. He warned Dave, though, that a comeback might not happen. Others tried to talk Dave out of the whole thing, suggesting that he consider retirement.

Dave worked hard. He could pitch—a little. He didn't have anything close to his old stuff, but at least he was trying.

And then a new and greater disaster struck. Marathoners speak of "hitting the wall." About 20 miles into a 26-mile marathon, a runner will reach a point of no return. All strength is gone. He feels as if he can't go another step. He's all run out. In a similar sense, Dave had hit the wall. He'd improved to the point where he could throw the ball, but he had no precision, no power, and above all, no real strength. Pitching a ball a hundred times in a major-league game would be impossible. In fact, for him it was impossible for any kind of game, perhaps even Little League!

Some friends and family wanted him to explore other options. When a manager called to talk to Dave about coaching, it looked like a good opportunity. But Dave wouldn't even return the call. "Don't count me out yet, " he told his wife when she asked him to at least return the call. They were words spoken partly in frustration and partly in faith that there was still something ahead.

His so-called comeback had turned into nothing but pain and frustration. Larry Brown told Dave at the clinic that there was nothing more he could do. Dave's arm was sore. He couldn't pitch as he once had. It looked like his pitching career was over. Dave spent his time in the dugout watching his teammates play, wishing and praying that somehow he might get into the fight again.

Then in June a point of no return occurred. Atlee Hammaker, another pitcher with the Giants and a fellow Christian, stood with Dave out in right field shagging flies. Dave felt the soreness coming on again in his arm, and he was afraid to try to throw. Atlee and he had been best friends a long time, though, and Atlee refused to accept Dave's fear. "Come on," he said, "let's play some catch."

Dave told him, "I don't know, Atlee. I think I'd better not."

"Hey," Atlee replied. "What have you got to lose? You've done your therapy. Your arm is strong. David, the time has come. Don't baby it any more. Let it rip. If it goes, it goes."

Dave finally relented. "All right," Atlee said, "let's throw through some of that pain. Just work through it. Let's air this baby out."[3]

Dave began to throw slow, then faster, then hard. He felt the ball "burrow in the air like a bullet." It began to whir, to sizzle. Dave was really throwing.

And his arm felt good.

What had happened? He didn't know. But he and Atlee played catch every day.

After that, Norm Sherry, the pitching coach, suggested Dave pitch batting practice. Dave tried and did okay. He went on the road with the team and began throwing batting practice regularly. Reporters began asking questions. Was this the guy who had cancer? In his pitching arm?

Yes.

Dave was getting better, and his arm wasn't sore at all. Maybe he really *was* coming back.

The next step was a simulated game in St. Louis on July 8. This was the kind of game where Giants played against Giants. But it was real play, with batters trying to hit as in a normal game, and pitchers trying to strike them out. Dave pitched 20 "pills" and stopped to rest. He ended up throwing three innings.

Now the reporting world was alive. This guy was returning to the big leagues!

The next hurdle was another simulated game of five innings. Dave pitched well from the start. Then, the last few pitches of the game, Dave "aired it out," firing his fastball in there at 85 miles per hour. Management pronounced Dave ready for the next step: the minors.

The Giants sent him to San Jose, and on July 23 Dave pitched for the San Jose Giants. His story had come alive. All of northern California seemed excited about this man who had battled a killer and won. A throng of 4,200 lined up two hours ahead of time to see this "miracle boy" pitch.

And pitch he did. Dave won the game, 2–0. A shut out! People cheered themselves hoarse. A comeback was in progress.

The second game in Reno, though, was the real miracle. During that game, Dave "locked in" mentally and physically with his pitching. He felt the old power. He was precise, accurate, right on the catcher's target. It was then that he knew he was back. Everywhere he went, there were reporters. How did he feel? How was his arm? Was he really coming back?

Dave moved up to triple A, pitching for the Phoenix Firebirds at an away game in Tucson, Arizona. There, Dave's pitching was even better. He pitched the whole game, gave up seven hits, and won, 3–2. Bob Kennedy, one of the Giants' top people in the front office, had come out to watch him pitch. After the win, Dave hurried back into the clubhouse; he wanted to call Al Rosen right away. He was ready to go back to the majors. But by the time he reached the office, Bob Kennedy was already on the phone. When Mr. Kennedy stepped back out, Dave had a pleading look on his face. Would he be going up?

"Pack your bags," Bob told him. "Get out of here. Get your flight to San Francisco first thing tomorrow. You're going to the big leagues."[4]

On August 10, 1989, San Francisco prepared an incredible welcome. Dave's story was all over the news. The whole world seemed to be rooting for this comeback kid. The giant board in center field at Candlestick Park lit up in monstrous letters: "Welcome back, Dave!"

Dravecky took the mound. Over 55,000 fans roared around him. He was about to do something no baseball player had ever done before. With only half a deltoid muscle in his pitching arm, Dave Dravecky meant to pitch in the major leagues. He would throw sliders, curves, and fastballs at some of the best batters on earth. Undoubtedly, many people just hoped he wouldn't have to hobble off the field, weak and undone. The crowd, though, was already giving him a standing ovation.

As Dave stood on the field near the mound, fans screaming around him, he prayed, "Thank you, Lord. Thank you for the privilege of doing this again. Thank you that you restored my arm so I could pitch. But most of all, thank you for what you've done for me. Thank you for saving me. Thank you for your love in Jesus Christ."[5]

Then he stepped on the pitching rubber and threw the first pitch. High and outside. Ball one. The crowd roared.

Second pitch. Fastball. High and inside. Luis Quinones of the Cincinnati Reds fouled it off down the third-base line. Another roar.

Third pitch. Backdoor slider. It caught the outside corner. Strike two. Dave knew he was way ahead of this batter.

Two more sliders and the count was 3–2.

Dave had to finish it. His first batter after a year-long comeback. That last pitch boiled in; another backdoor slider. It was right on the money. Quinones went after it and sliced a bit off the edge. A pop fly. One out.

The crowd roared its approval. They were on their feet again. The adrenaline was pumping in Dave Dravecky. The next two batters went down in succession. As Dave ran into the dugout, the crowd stood, cheered, and clapped. Another standing ovation.

WELCOME BACK, DAVE!

It went that way through seven innings. The Giants scored several runs, too, and it was 4–0. A comeback shutout?

But in the seventh inning, Dave began having control problems. No one noticed, but Dave knew it. He could easily get into trouble in the next inning.

In the eighth, Dave allowed the first batter to get a broken-bat single. He could lose the game, he knew now. Soon, he had put two on base and then he handed Luis Quinones a pearl. He knocked it out of the park. The crowd was silent. Suddenly, San Francisco's 4–0 lead was cut to 4–3.

It could end up a loss. But when Dave went into the dugout, the stadium gave him another standing ovation.

Dave didn't pitch the top of the ninth. Steve Bedrosian, the Giants' "stopper," went out to the mound. Immediately, the crowd went wild. Another standing ovation. Terry Kennedy, Dave's friend and catcher, yelled at Dave in the dugout, "Go on out there. It's your day. Take a bow."

Dave was embarrassed, but he finally went out.

As if that wasn't enough, the crowd wouldn't stop. It looked like a win for a man in his first time out after nearly a year on the sidelines.

There were over fourteen standing ovations that day. In the end, Dave racked up a win with Bedrosian bringing the Giants home. Dave Dravecky had come back. And with real fireworks!

In the locker room, Dave again had a chance to share his faith before the cameras and the world. "It's important for me to give credit where credit is due," he said. "I want to give praise and glory to Jesus Christ for allowing me the opportunity to come back and play again."[6] He thanked his doctors, friends, therapists, and family, then answered numerous questions. It was one of the most inspiring, startling, and unrepeatable comebacks in baseball history.

Unfortunately, it was not to last. In Dave's next game, against the Montreal Expos on August 15, his humerus snapped. With a broken arm, he was out of the majors for the season, and it ended up for good. The story was all over the news. His comeback had ended. Nearly a year later the cancer returned, and Dave lost his whole left arm.

Still, today, Dave writes,

I leave baseball with a great sense of satisfaction. When I think back on my career, I do so with a

big, fat smile on my face. How could I feel anything else?

Every year in America hundreds of thousands of
kids go out to play Little League, and every year
each of them dreams of playing in the major
leagues. The odds are so slim. It's as if you had a
huge stadium jammed full of kids, each wearing a
uniform and a glove, and just one out of all those
thousands got picked to come down onto the field
and play with the big boys.

I was that kid. I got to play with the big boys.

And even more: I got the chance to come back.[7]

It was a gift of God born in struggle, pain, hard
work, and determination. But a gift, just the same,
that the Lord of Dave Dravecky rejoiced to give.

You can read more about Dave Dravecky in *Today's Heroes: Dave Dravecky.*

1. Dave Dravecky with Tim Stafford, *Comeback* (Grand Rapids: Zondervan, 1990), 93.
2. Dravecky, 98.
3. Dravecky, 153–54.
4. Dravecky, 172.
5. Dravecky, 180.
6. Dravecky, 187.
7. Dravecky, 249.

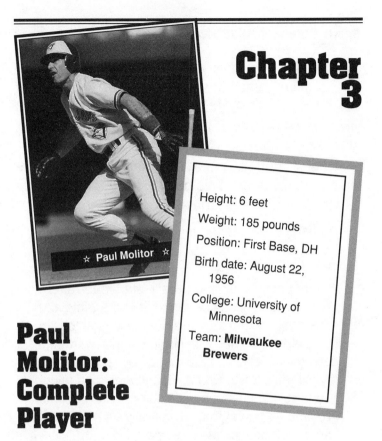

Chapter 3

☆ Paul Molitor ☆

Height: 6 feet

Weight: 185 pounds

Position: First Base, DH

Birth date: August 22, 1956

College: University of Minnesota

Team: **Milwaukee Brewers**

Paul Molitor: Complete Player

Paul Molitor holds some big records. On July 26, 1987, he stole three bases in one inning—a major-league record. On October 12, 1982, while playing for the Milwaukee Brewers, he hit five singles in a World Series game—the record for both hits and singles in a single World Series game. In July and August of 1987, he hit safely in 39 straight games. That streak commanded a lot of attention as

Paul was going after Joe DiMaggio's record 56-consecutive-game hitting streak set in 1941. Then in 1992, he batted .320, the fourth-highest average that year for the American League. He has been named an all-star six times.

Paul is a humble man of whom some say there isn't "a phony bone in his body." He became a Christian in college at the University of Minnesota:

> It wasn't until I started my junior year at the University of Minnesota that I really got in touch with God.
>
> At that point in my life, I really started to realize my need for Christ. I began to read the Bible and think about Him a lot more. I gave myself to Him then. But I struggled with some spiritual warfare. I don't think Satan wanted me to get serious about my commitment to Christ. I found that I was reluctant to surrender some of the things I had become involved in, things that were really bad for me—some drug abuse, late-night partying, etc.
>
> But through God's persistent love, I was able to give myself up to Him.[1]

One of eight children in his family, Paul had a strong moral upbringing. His mother and father have supported him every step of the way. He has shared his faith with thousands of people and fans, speaking for the Fellowship of Christian Athletes frequently. He says, "The Lord means everything to me.

I don't know how anyone can face each day not having that foundation."[2]

But Paul Molitor has also made some mistakes. In 1984, a cocaine dealer was put on trial in Milwaukee. It was revealed that Paul had been one of his customers back in 1981. At first Paul refused to answer questions by reporters. Perhaps he didn't know how to handle it. He was a hero to many young people, and his virtues were regularly written about in the press. His Christian testimony was well known.

But in the end, Paul realized that the biblical path of confession and forgiveness was the right way. He came clean. In an article in *Sports Illustrated*, he said, "In '81 I was injured and not traveling. I used bad judgment a few times. It's all very much in the past."[3]

In 1987, Paul experienced one of the highlights of his baseball career. As designated hitter for the Brewers, he got at least one hit in 39 consecutive games. This ranks as the fifth-longest streak in modern times (since 1900), behind Ty Cobb's 40, George Sisler's 41, Pete Rose's 44 (in 1978), and of course, the greatest of all, Joe DiMaggio's amazing 56-game streak in 1941, just before the United States entered World War II. Paul's streak bettered the Brewers' record of 24 consecutive games set by Dave May in 1973. It is also the longest hitting streak of the 1980s.

The streak began on July 16, 1987, with a 1-for-4 showing against the California Angels. (Joe DiMaggio's streak also began with a 1-for-4 performance.) Paul had just come off the disabled list. In fact, he had been so plagued by injuries the last few years that he'd missed over 200 games. Over his career he has suffered from "a pulled rib cage muscle, torn ligaments in an ankle and an elbow, a sprained ankle, a torn hamstring, a dislocated finger, an impinged shoulder, a fractured knuckle, and a broken thumb."[4]

Of course, no one noticed the streak till Paul got into double digits. "I once had a 17-game streak," Paul said. "When I got to 15 or 16 this time, I realized I had a chance to better that. Then the next big number was the team record. A lot of the pressure went after I passed that."[5]

The streak almost came to end several times when Paul went into the ninth inning hitless. One of the most dramatic ninth innings came in Baltimore when he was shooting for his twenty-seventh straight hit. With the count at 1 and 0, Paul ripped a fastball over the left-field fence. Paul said, "I had been struggling in that game. I'd swung the bat more like a guy with a 27-game hitless streak."[6] At the 31-game mark, he was hitting .411 with 53 hits in 129 at bats for the streak. He also had 6 home runs, 26 RBI, 34 runs, and an amazing 15 stolen bases—one more sign that he goes all out whenever he's on the field.

It broke Paul's heart when he was traded from the Milwaukee Brewers in 1992. He had spent his whole baseball career with the Brewers: fifteen seasons. In his last two seasons as a Brewer, he hit .325 and .320. But the Brewers couldn't offer him the contract he wanted, and as a free agent he could shop around. The Blue Jays stepped in and offered him $13 million over three seasons. He couldn't turn that down. Reluctantly, Paul headed for Toronto.

Paul had one of his best seasons in 1993. After the all-star break (he was on the team), he batted .361 for the Blue Jays and ended the season at .332. He powered 22 home runs (a career high) and knocked in 111 RBI. He normally plays DH (designated hitter) for the Blue Jays now, and that helped him have an injury-free season, but he wields a capable glove at first and third bases as well. In fact, during the World Series he played at both positions with no errors. In the last three seasons no one has had more hits or runs than Molitor, although he has not led the league in either of those categories in any single season.

Even though the hero shot of the 1993 World

Series belonged to Joe Carter with his ninth-inning Series-winning home run, the Fall Classic was Paul's all the way. He was selected MVP after the final game, and it's no wonder. His hitting surprised everyone but those close to him.

Paul's swing is what makes him such a number-one hitter year in and year out. *Sports Illustrated* said, "He has cut down his swing to a nearly perfect, economical motion. He holds his hands still until the last possible moment; then, with 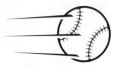 virtually no stride, he attacks the baseball with a quick, powerful stabbing action."[7] In the American League Championship Series that swing bought him six straight hits, another record. In the World Series itself he batted .500, going 12 for 24. He also scored 10 runs and accumulated 24 total bases. Even for him, it's an astounding record. He just keeps hitting. Cito Gaston, the manager of the Blue Jays, calls him "the best-kept secret in baseball."

At 37, Molitor is an "older" player, but that doesn't mean he lets up. In the third game of the 1993 World Series, Toronto was six runs up. It was nearing one o'clock in the morning, and everyone was beat when Paul whacked a grounder to shortstop. It was deep, and Paul knew there was a chance for a single. Paul churned his legs faster than ever and made it.

And Joe Carter didn't hit the only homer in that dramatic sixth game. Paul blasted a 393-foot shot to move Toronto to a 5–1 lead. As he rounded second base, he considered doing some theatrics. Maybe a little jig or a high five or something. But he caught his father's eyes in the stands, and that stopped him. He didn't want to make the Phillies feel too bad, so he just jogged along with no dramatics. It's his "respect for the game" that drives him to be such a gentleman.

Paul was also the third batter in that fated ninth inning of Game Six. Rickey Henderson had got on base with a walk and the second batter had flown out to left field. The Blue Jays were down by one run, and even if they lost this game, they still had one more to go. But wouldn't it be nice . . .

Paul's thought was that if he crushed a home run, the Blue Jays would win the game and the Series and he would go down in history. But immediately he pulled the thought back. He thought, "No, play the percentages. Keep the rally moving."[8]

That's the perfect team player. Paul's not one to go for fame and glory. No, going all out in the crunch no matter what the score is what it's all about. He said, "Baseball can sell itself if it's played right. You play it the same way whether it's the playoffs, the World Series or the preseason. I've had enough baseball taken away from me, so even grounding out is not that bad."[9]

That same night, after Joe Carter smashed his Series-ending home run, Paul wept with joy right there on the field. He had wanted this ever since he was traded from the Brewers, who lost the World Series in 1982. Paul had always wanted to win a World Championship. The Blue Jays had won it the year before he came to Toronto, so he had his hopes up. Everyone on the team knew how he'd played in that 1982 Series, with five hits in a single game. All the Blue Jays wanted to give the World Series to Paul, who, at 37, was a kind of "elder statesman" and designated leader of the team. Joe Carter threw his arms around Paul's neck and said, "This is for you!" Perhaps it was just a little more of the faith they both share.

That World Series was a climax for Molitor. Twelve hits, including a home run. A .500 batting average. Ten runs scored. Twenty-four total bases. He was moved at the fact that so many of his team- mates expressed how much it meant to them to see him win. Al Leiter, a Toronto pitcher, said, "We've had so much success here that people begin to think, 'When are we going to play, and who are we going to beat.' Then he comes here after all he's been through, and you see how precious winning is."[10]

After the World Series was won, Paul said, "I def- initely respect the game, and that's why I felt a somberness, a stillness, knowing how long I'd waited to feel that. It was everything I imagined. Days and weeks and months from now, I'm sure it will grow deeper in meaning. But right now I'm very peaceful with it. Yes, you get excited, and there's a rush of adrenaline. But there's something very peaceful about it."[11]

It was a precious win for him, something that will only deepen with the years. The same way faith in Christ does.

---

1. Bill Alexson, *Batting a Thousand* (Nashville: Nelson, 1990), 106–7.
2. Dave Branon and Joe Pellegrino, *Safe at Home* (Chicago: Moody, 1992), 305.
3. Morin Bishop, "More Than Halfway There," *Sports Illustrated,* 24 August 1987, 27.
4. Tom Verducci, "The Complete Player," *Sports Illustrated,* 1 November 1993, 29.
5. Bishop, 29.
6. Bishop, 29.
7. Verducci, 29.
8. Verducci, 31.
9. Verducci, 28.
10. Verducci, 31.
11. Verducci, 28.

☆ Greg Gagne ☆

Height: 5 feet, 11 inches

Weight: 172 pounds

Position: Shortstop

Birth date: November 12, 1961

Team: **Minnesota Twins**

Chapter 4

Greg Gagne: No Errors

Not many guys have to spend seven years in the minors to make it to the big leagues. By your seventh year, you've usually found something else to do. Maybe selling stocks. Or insurance. Maybe you've gone to school, gotten a degree, and become an accountant or something else. The fact is, most guys don't hang in there that long. If they don't make the majors in two or three or four years, they're done. The lark is over.

In his sixth year in the minors, though, playing for Toledo, Greg Gagne was invited to the big time—the "Show." He went up to the majors for ten games, hit .111, and was sent back down. Disappointment swirled in his mind, but at least he'd been there.

In 1984 he went up again. This time for two games. He batted once and made an out. He went back to the minors.

Still, Greg was a good player; a shortstop who made few errors and hit in the upper .200s most of his minor-league career. So in 1985, the Minnesota Twins brought him up to the mother club. He batted .225 that year, hit two home runs, and played well in 114 games. The Twins needed a regular shortstop, so they decided to keep him. He would end up playing for the Twins in two World Series and doing some remarkable things in each one.

Greg didn't get a great start in life, either. He grew up in Somerset, Massachusetts, one of nine children. When he was eleven, his parents decided to get a divorce. It tore Greg up, and in a short time he slipped into the standard temptations of life: drugs and drinking. He was an excellent ball player, but off the diamond his life was a mess. He skipped school a lot and didn't care about anything, much less himself. Many of his friends thought of him as "Most Likely to Waste His Life," not as someone who would play in two World Series.

Greg was even expelled from the ball team one year, though he had talent. He began drinking himself to death. On one occasion, he flipped his car over and hung upside down, barely able to breathe, ready to choke on his own vomit. He was headed for hell.

But Greg's father wouldn't give up on his son. He brought him into his house and decided to raise him with an iron hand. Greg also drew confidence from several coaches who told him he had talent and could end up in the big leagues. Although his high school days were a testing time, he made it through them with his dad's and coaches' support.

Greg decided to go to Murray State University in Kentucky and even signed a letter of intent. But the New York Yankees had also noticed him. They offered him a contract to play on a class-A team in Paintsville, Kentucky. He decided to go. College could wait.

While Greg was playing well on the class-A team and getting noticed, Greg's mother also continued to show interest in his development. She gave him a book to read written by a noted preacher. He found that it was

49

"talking about this faith and this God I did not know. It said that with God, all things are possible. That kind of planted a seed in my life."[1]

Greg kept thinking about the idea of faith and God. The next summer, the Yankees moved Greg up to double-A ball. On a bus ride, he noticed several teammates reading the Bible and talking in a front seat. He walked up and started to listen. Soon he got into the discussion. Greg found himself agreeing with what they were talking about. It was real to him. The Bible's words struck him as true, and he knew that he needed to do something about it.

At a motel in Greensboro, North Carolina, Greg threw himself on his bed and cried out to God. "I wept like I had never wept before. I confessed all of my sins and asked Christ—this God that I really didn't even know—to come into my life. And He did. That's when I was born again. I let Jesus Christ into my life, and that's when my new life started. That's when things really changed for me."[2]

Although Greg ran on a spiritual high those first few weeks, reality soon set in. Problems piled up. Things went wrong. The biggest problem was environment. He was playing ball in Orlando, Florida, and it was terribly hot during those steamy afternoons in the park. Soon, Greg wanted to quit. When his dad arrived to watch him play, Greg complained, "Dad, it's too hot. I can't play down here."

His father responded, "Well, what are you going to do, go home? Then what? What are you going to do back home?"

Suddenly, Greg realized he was qualified for little more than dishwashing, waiting tables, and tough construction jobs. He realized his love was baseball. He decided to tough it out. In a short time, he was breaking records—including most assists, at bats, home runs, and RBI by a shortstop.[3] Before long, he was moved to Toledo, a triple-A team, and from there to Minnesota in 1985. He was 23 years old.

Greg's first full season with the Twins was 1986. He played in 156 games, almost every game of the season. In 472 at bats, he logged 118 hits, including twelve home runs, for a .250 average. Though not considered a power hitter, he was consistent and filled the lower half of the Twins' lineup admirably. He made few errors on the field too, becoming a fine defensive player.

In 1987, the Twins mounted a strong offensive season, won 85 games, and went to the World Series. Greg had a good season that year, batting .265 in 437 at bats. He had ten home runs, but he played only 137 games. He'd gone 0 for 30 in hitting that September, and he came into the World Series against the St. Louis Cardinals in a partial slump. Though he continued to play all right, he was far from spectacular.

The Twins had been known as the "Twinkies" in

previous years, unable to put together a World Series season. But something called the "Homer Hankie," a special handkerchief designed by the local newspaper to put some spirit into the crowd, had captivated the fans. Often during a game, when a power hitter like Kirby Puckett stepped to the plate, fans yelled and waved Homer Hankies by the thousands.

That 1987 Series was a real tango between the Cardinals and the Twins. Both teams won all three of their home games and came into Game Seven tied. The last game was played in the Hubert H. Humphrey Metrodome. Fans waved their Homer Hankies and screamed through the whole game. Some of the players wore earplugs, the noise was so great.

St. Louis rapped out four singles in the second inning to log the first two runs of the game. Those would be their only runs of the game, and they got only two more hits during the next six innings.

A bad call at the plate canceled a possible run for the Twins in the second inning. They did score one run, though, on an RBI single by Steve Lombardozzi. In the fifth, Kirby Puckett smacked a double, bringing in the tying run.

Then came the sixth inning. The St. Louis pitcher lost control on the first two batters and walked them both. Another walk, and the bases were loaded. Then two quick outs made it look like a lost inning. Greg Gagne came to the plate. Homer Hankies were everywhere. This was his chance at a World Series grand slam!

Greg took a few pitches and swung at a couple, pushing the count to 3–2. It didn't look good.

The pitcher took the open stance, regarded the runners, then threw. Greg whacked the ball down the third-base line. The Cardinals' Tom Lawless leaped and stabbed at the ball. He got it, but had no time to tag third. He went for first.

Greg was fast. He beat the throw and a run scored. The winning run.

No one knew it was the winning run then, of course, but Greg had come through. He'd made the clutch hit, and it was that run that won the World Series in 1987. The hit was as valuable as Joe Carter's homer in the ninth inning of the 1993 World Series, because it scored the winning run—and that's all that counts.

Greg was to have an even bigger hit for the Twins in 1991. Although it didn't start off to be a good year—Greg went 0 for 32 in June, a major slump— he finally pulled out of it and didn't suffer another slump all summer. He batted .265 that year, the same as 1987 (they are his second- and third-best batting years behind the .272 he notched in 1989). He played in 139 games with 408 at bats and 108 hits. He swatted eight home runs that year, far from his best, but offered a major contribution to a team that would again go to the Series.

The year had something else to celebrate as well. Greg put in 76 consecutive errorless innings that summer, the second-longest errorless-inning streak for a shortstop in American League history (Cal Ripken, Jr., has the longest: 95 straight innings). The streak ended on a short-hopping ball that Greg had to charge. He knew he shouldn't throw to first—the runner had it beat—but he decided to go for it anyway. He overthrew first. It was a small mental error, but costly. The streak was over, now just another memory among many.

The biggest moment of 1991 came in the fifth inning of Game One of the World Series: the Twins versus the Braves. Both teams struggled to get the upper hand. The Twins led, 1–0. Two men got on, and Greg Gagne came to the plate. Homer Hankies were once again being waved throughout the park.

Greg was eager to hit because he had struck out his first time up. The pitcher served up a change-up on the first pitch, catching Greg off guard. He swung and missed; his timing was way off.

Telling himself to stay back on the next pitch and look to drive the ball into the hole, Greg readied himself. This time the pitcher fired heat: the fastball. Greg leaned back and whammed it over the fence. Everyone just stood there looking at it. It was gone! Home run. Three big runs scored.

Suddenly, the Twins had a four-run lead in the first game. They would ultimately win the game, 5–2. Greg says that home run "was the biggest hit of my career."

And to what does Greg Gagne credit this World Series home run? Greg credits his success at baseball to his walk with Jesus Christ. He says, "I look at the younger kids . . . the ones who look up to us and really think something of us. . . . I can influence them more in the way I walk than in what I say."[4]

Greg has had an influence on his fellow players, too. Gary Gaetti, another Twins' Christian, went through a rough time in 1988 after ripping the cartilage in his left knee. Surgery followed, and he was in bed and on crutches for a while. When Gary arrived back at team headquarters to report for duty, he found several players, including Greg, talking about Jesus Christ coming back to earth for "His team" at the end of human history. Gary asked to see the book they had been reading. It was the Bible. Gary decided that he, too, wanted to be on God's team.

"I just emptied my mind and heart to God and asked Him to save me," Gary says. "He did, and I've begun to have a great understanding of His Word. The addictions I had to drinking and TV were washed away. The wrong thoughts and attitudes were removed. I don't seek the things of this world anymore."[5]

Today some pro teams have as many Christians

as non-Christians because of the witness of guys like Gary and Greg. But Greg still gets put down sometimes by fellow players for maintaining his faith. Once he found a sign on his locker that said "Get drunk and be somebody." However, Greg has been through that kind of rebellion and knows it's not for him. He says, "I had already done that and being on drugs and running away from home and skipping classes. I don't have to do those things because I know who I am in Christ Jesus, that I am a new man now."[6]

With such an outlook, how can Greg help but continue to win and serve and gain the applause and approval of all those young people he cares so much about?

1. Dave Branon and Joe Pellegrino, *Safe at Home* (Chicago: Moody, 1992), 115.
2. Branon and Pellegrino, 116.
3. Branon and Pellegrino, 117.
4. Branon and Pellegrino, 120.
5. Bill Alexson, *Batting a Thousand* (Nashville: Nelson, 1990), 41.
6. Alexson, 121.

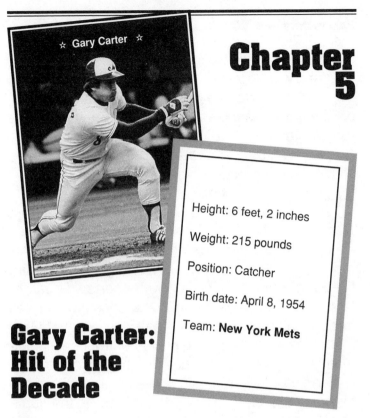

★ Gary Carter ★

Chapter 5

Height: 6 feet, 2 inches

Weight: 215 pounds

Position: Catcher

Birth date: April 8, 1954

Team: **New York Mets**

Gary Carter: Hit of the Decade

For years Gary Carter's dream had been to clobber a game-winning home run in the World Series. He imagined himself a sure-batting Mickey Mantle stepping up to the plate and hefting one into the stands before a roaring crowd.

But sometimes a single at crunch time in the World Series is just as crucial to a team as a homer. Consider what happened in the 1986 Series between the New York Mets and the Boston Red Sox.

The Mets were trailing the Red Sox in the Series, 3–2, and were down 5–3 in the tenth inning of Game Six. Two outs. No one on. Two strikes. It was do-or-die time, and Gary Carter stood at the plate. A home run wouldn't win the game. An out would end the Series right then and there. But a hit—any hit—would keep the team alive.

What does Gary do?

Stay tuned while we fill you in on a little about Gary.

Gary had been troubled by the death of his mother in 1966 when he was twelve, and he had filled the emptiness he felt with sports. His father took over the role of mother and coached Gary all through Little League and then Pony League. Gary started as a shortstop and pitcher until a coach spotted his "rifle" arm and suggested he try catching.

Gary started professional baseball at age eighteen. He signed with the Expos in 1973, the same year he accepted Christ through the influence of his roommate, another catcher named John Boccabella.

He tells the story this way:

> I spent nearly two years in the minors, but it was there that I made the greatest discovery of my life. I went to spring training in 1973, and a catcher for the Expos named John Boccabella sort of took me under his wing. He was a Christian, and he got me going to church with him and started answering my questions about religion. I

saw in John an inner peace and happiness that I wanted, and he said it could only have come through a personal relationship with Jesus Christ.

A few weeks later I was sent back to the minors, which seemed to be a setback for me. One night while lying in bed, I just started talking to the Lord and told Him I needed Him and wanted Him to be my personal Savior. I also told Him I wanted to live for Him and be able to share His Word. As I look back now, I realize it was the greatest decision of my life.[1]

By the age of 20, Gary had worked his way into a starting position with the Expos. Few catchers go a full schedule of games in the big leagues because of the double punishment they take on their catching hand and their knees, so Gary played partly in the outfield and partly as catcher.

Montreal was in the cellar Gary's first few years. But by 1977, behind Gary's catching and hitting, the Expos had moved up. Gary smashed his way to a .284 batting average, with 31 home runs and 84 RBI.

In 1981, Gary led the Expos to the National League playoffs. Then a Dodger home run with two outs in the ninth inning of the final game sent the Expos packing. They'd come close, but not close enough.

Gary had wanted to play his entire career as an Expo, as Ernie Banks had done with the Cubs or

Carl Yastrzemski with the Red Sox. However, in 1985 the Expos needed to make some changes. They decided to trade their seven-time all-star catcher to the Mets.

Gary and the Mets did well their first year together: They finished second in their division. But 1986 would be their year. And Gary's.

The Mets went 108–54 that year, the best record in the team's history. Behind the pitching of Bobby Ojeda and Dwight Gooden, they finished first in their division, with their closest rival, the Phillies, coming in 21 games behind them. They were on their way to the World Series. But first they had to get through the Houston Astros for the league championship.

In the bottom of the twelfth of Game Five of the playoffs, with the series knotted at two-all, and the score 1–1, Gary stepped up to the plate. He had gone 1 for 21 in this series against the Astros, but he was swinging the bat well; he simply hadn't connected for anything significant. Two men were on base, with one out. Darryl Strawberry had just said to him, "All you need is a little base hit, Kid. Don't worry about it."[2] (Gary's nickname on the team was "Kid.") Gary's family were sitting in the stands, and the camera had just zoomed in on them.

Charlie Kerfeld stood on the mound for the Astros. He threw three quick balls to Gary. But Gary wanted to hit, not walk. He had to break out of his slump. He peered down at the third-base coach. The coach gave the signal: "take it."

Kerfeld served up Gary's first strike.

Gary looked at third base. "Hit away" was the signal. He settled in, but fouled it off. Two more pitches. Two more fouls. Gary was still alive. He'd gotten a piece of the ball; now for the whole banana.

The next pitch was low and away, and Gary got all of it. It was a one-hopper up the middle—a base hit. As Gary ran for first, he saw the man who had been on second make it home. The game was over. Gary Carter had knocked home the game-winning run.

The dugout emptied as happy Mets embraced Gary on the field. He saw his wife and family in the stands, laughing and crying at the same time. Relief. 2 for 22—but what a two!

Then came Game Six of the playoffs against the Astros. The Mets were now leading the series, 3–2. It would be a game of games, in a season of seasons.

The game went along smoothly enough. Gary batted three times and got zip. He was 2 for 25. The Astros led, 3–0 going into the ninth, but then the Mets scored three quick runs. The game was now tied up.

Each team added a run in the fourteenth inning. By the sixteenth the game was still locked, 4–4. Darryl Strawberry knocked a high, short fly to center that the fielder lost in the Astrodome roof. Strawberry got two bases. Then Ray Knight banged out a quick single that sent Darryl home. Knight ended up on second base. Next came a walk and two wild pitches, and Knight ran home. The Mets were now two runs ahead, 6–4, with a runner at second. Lenny Dykstra swatted the next ball into right field for a single that sent another runner home. The Mets ended the inning leading 7–4. The Astros came up to the plate ready for war.

The Astros quickly scored two runs and put a base runner on first. Jesse Orosco was pitching for the Mets. He was tired, and his fastball was getting knocked all over the place. Gary had several conferences on the mound with Jesse, and the two agreed they needed to pitch something instead of the fastball. Orosco's pitch was the slider. They had to try it. Men were on first and second. The score was 7–6.

Kevin Bass came to the plate. He had been blasting the Mets all through the series. Gary figured he was looking for a fastball to slam into the upper deck, so he called for a slider. Orosco threw it. Strike. Another slider. Strike two. And another. And another. They weren't even good pitches, but Bass

was swinging at them anyway. The count went to 3 and 2.

Gary called for one more slider. It sailed in. The batter swung.

Out!

The game was over, and the Mets were going to the World Series. Gary had called for the right pitches, the primary job of the catcher, and he had every reason to be proud.

In the World Series, the Mets would face the Boston Red Sox: Roger Clemens, Wade Boggs, Carlton Fisk, Dwight Evans, Jim Rice, Marty Barrett—a powerful lineup and pitching staff. They would be formidable. Gary got ready to do some hitting. He'd gone 4 for 27 in the playoffs, getting two hits in that thrilling sixth game. He believed that his slump was over. Now he needed to do something—something big!

Still, it had to be a team effort, and, if anything, Gary is a team player. He's no loner. While at Montreal, he often gave away clothing or other products to his teammates from advertisements he was involved in. At one point, just to create a better atmosphere, he spent his own money to buy director's chairs for every team member with their nicknames on the back flap.

The Mets at that time were a close club, and Gary had built friendships with several of his teammates. His Christian testimony was strong too. He often spoke to young people, even going into prisons and speaking to young inmates. "I feel a role model is very important," he says. "It gives the kids an opportunity to follow someone and look up to him and maybe direct themselves in the same capacity for the future for their lives. . . . I think it's important to take that responsibility because the kids of today are going to be the superstars of the future."[3]

The World Series didn't start too well for the Mets. Playing in their home park, Shea Stadium, they dropped the first game, 1–0, in a pitchers' duel. And in the second game they got shelled, 9–3. The Mets went into the third game at Fenway Park in Boston with grim determination. They had to win twice in Fenway, or there would be no going back to New York.

The third game started with a bang. Lenny Dykstra homered and Gary doubled to give the Mets a 4–0 first-inning lead. In the seventh, Gary lined over third baseman Wade Boggs's head. Base hit! Now Gary *knew* his slump was over, and so was the Mets' losing streak. They took the game away, 7–1. No contest.

The Mets went into the fourth game looking to tie the Series. In his second time up, in the fourth inning, Gary crushed a fastball into left field for a home run. He was almost dancing as he ran around the bases in a half trot.

In Gary's third at bat, in the sixth, he racked up another hit: a double. Now he was cruising. Then in the eighth, Gary struck fire again. He got two quick strikes, fouled one off, and then got a fat, hanging curve. He smacked it hard, so hard it was gone before he reached first base.

What is better than hitting a homer in your first World Series? Hitting two! The score ended 6–1, and the Mets and Red Sox were tied at two games each.

Game Five was a battle: Dwight Gooden against Bruce Hurst. A pitching duel. Gary went hitless in four times at bat. The final score: 4–2, Sox. The Red Sox led the Series, 3–2. The Mets had to win the next game or it was over.

Now the immortal Game Six—the game where Gary would stand at the plate in that do-or-die situation. Roger Clemens was pitching against Bobby Ojeda, both all-stars.

The Red Sox scored one run in each of the first two innings, then nothing for two innings. The Mets came back in the fourth and tied it up, 2–2. In the seventh inning, the Red Sox scored another run. In the eighth, the Mets tied it up on a hard line drive by Gary into left field that scored a man from third. Another RBI for the Mets' all-star catcher. It was looking like Gary Carter might end up with the MVP award if this kept up.

At the end of the ninth it was 3–3. Extra innings. In the tenth, the Red Sox struck fire. Dave Henderson, their center fielder, led off with a home run. The Mets' pitcher, Rick Aguilera, struck out the next two, but Wade Boggs connected for a double. Then Marty Barrett, who was hitting close to .500 for the Series, punched a line drive into center for a base hit and brought Boggs home. It was 5–3. It looked like the Series was over.

Bottom of the tenth. The Mets had to do something. The first two batters flew out to right and center. And Gary Carter came to the plate with two outs, no one on base, and the World Series at stake. Gary says, "I felt a presence in me, or perhaps beside me, a calming certainty that I wasn't alone. I was not alone, and I was not, so help me, going to make the last out of the World Series. I felt certain of that. It would have been unacceptable, impossible; I would have lived with it all winter, and probably beyond. It might have stalked me for the rest of my career."[4]

There could not have been more pressure on a man than was on Gary Carter at that moment. Calvin Schiraldi, the Red Sox closer and ace, was pitching. He blew in a fastball; Gary fouled it back. Then he threw another fastball right under Gary's chin. Ball one. Next pitch. Outside. Another ball. Gary was ahead of him, 2–1.

The next pitch was a fastball too, only this time Gary drove it into left field for a single. The Mets were still alive! It wasn't the home run Gary had dreamed about, but he had kept the Mets in the running when an out would have meant their death in the Series. It was the most important single of the World Series at that point—and of Gary's life.

Kevin Mitchell came up next, pinch-hitting for Aguilera. He was a rookie, and it was the most important at bat of his life too. He smacked the ball into center. Another hit. Runners at first and second.

Then it was Ray Knight. The count went to 0–2. Schiraldi was way ahead of him. The next ball was a fastball, inside. Knight connected on the handle, knocking it over the second baseman's head. Another hit, and Gary Carter scored from second. Now it was 5–4, with runners at first and third.

John McNamara, the Red Sox manager, called for reliever Bob Stanley; Schiraldi was done. What was happening to the Red Sox was incredible, impossible. How could they lose this game now?

Mookie Wilson, the Mets' left fielder, took the first pitch for a called strike. The second pitch, though, got past Rich Gedman, the catcher, and Kevin Mitchell came home. Suddenly, the score was tied, 5–5. The Mets were going crazy; the stadium roared like a million crazed wolves. This was glory!

Wilson kept fouling off pitches. Finally he swatted a grounder to the Red Sox first baseman, Bill Buckner.

The grounder to Buckner. Maybe you've seen it. It's the stuff of legend. A simple little grounder, but Buckner missed it! In the World Series. When the game was almost won. It trickled off into right field, and Ray Knight came around third hard. No one was even near the ball. Knight roared in and it was over: 6–5, Mets. The tide had turned.

The last game of the World Series was almost anticlimactic, even though it was a great game. The Mets won it 8–5, and won the Series. The season was Gary Carter's "dream season," and he would go on to write a book by that title. In the parade that ended at City Hall in New York City giving the Mets their final hurrah, some of the Mets had a chance to speak. Gary Carter just said one thing: "Thank you for helping to make the dream come true."[5]

1. Bill Alexson, *Batting a Thousand* (Nashville: Nelson, 1990), 44–45.
2. Gary Carter and John Hough Jr., *A Dream Season* (New York: Harcourt, Brace, Jovanovich, 1987), 43.
3. Carter and Hough, 83.
4. Carter and Hough, 176.
5. Carter and Hough, 210.

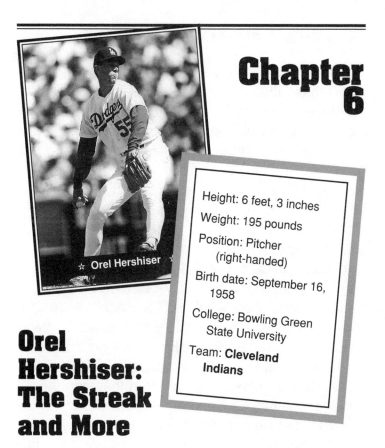

☆ Orel Hershiser ☆

Height: 6 feet, 3 inches

Weight: 195 pounds

Position: Pitcher (right-handed)

Birth date: September 16, 1958

College: Bowling Green State University

Team: **Cleveland Indians**

Orel Hershiser: The Streak and More

In 1968, Don Drysdale, pitcher for the Los Angeles Dodgers and now a member of the Baseball Hall of Fame, pitched five consecutive shutouts. All told, he logged fifty-eight and two-thirds straight innings without allowing a single run to score.

In 1988, another Dodger named Orel Hershiser finished his season racing after that supposedly unreachable mark.

69

Orel's story is not your typical superstar tale. He didn't make the varsity baseball team of his Cherry Hill, New Jersey, high school till his junior year. Then he pitched and played shortstop. He wasn't a bad hitter, but he was far from the best player on the team.

When Orel left for Bowling Green State University in Ohio in 1976, he wasn't ready for college. That first year he almost flunked out. He started hitchhiking back to Cherry Hill for support and encouragement, but only made it to a hotel in mid-Pennsylvania. There he finally called his parents and told them what was going on. They didn't yell at him; they counseled him to enroll in summer school back at Bowling Green and to make something of himself.

Orel did, and this time he passed his classes with ease. He also played on the team that won the All American Amateur Baseball Association championship in the United States. His sophomore year he got his fastball up another five miles per hour, finished the season with a 6–2 pitching record, and made the all-conference team.

In 1979, Orel decided to enter the amateur baseball draft without first finishing college. He soon got a call that he had been drafted in the first round by the San Diego Padres. He was astonished. But when he told some friends about it and got a rather ho-hum response, he found out it was all a big joke:

The call hadn't been from San Diego, but Bowling Green. One of his baseball friends had set him up.

Still, Orel did manage to be drafted in the seventeenth round by the Dodgers. He wasn't yet 21 (his father had to co-sign the contract), but the Dodgers gave him $10,000 for signing, and he was sent to a class-A club in Clinton, Iowa. It was there that Orel met Butch Wickensheimer. Butch read his Bible nearly constantly during off hours, and Orel was soon asking him questions. In a way, he wanted to get an answer that was clearly contradictory, so that he could write off the Bible, Christ, and Christianity for good. But even though Butch's answers weren't perfect, Orel couldn't shake the fact that they did make sense.

When he went home at the end of the season, Orel dug out his personal Bible from the bottom drawer of his dresser. He had attended church at Easter and Christmas most of his life, but there had never been anything real in it; it was just something you did.

But Butch was different, and Orel couldn't seem to get him out of his mind. He had gone 4–0 that year and was feeling pretty good about baseball. When both he and Butch were invited to attend the Arizona Instructional League that fall he asked to room with Butch.

More questions. More answers. More thinking. The thing that most intrigued Orel was something

Butch kept telling him, "God loves you. God wants a relationship with you forever. Jesus is the answer."

Deep down, Orel knew it was his decision. Butch couldn't give him the relationship or hand him eternal life. He had to accept Christ personally.

Then one night in September, Orel relates, "I was the only one in the room. I pulled out the Gideon Bible and was reading the book of John. My mind was racing. Do I believe in God? Yes. Do I believe the Bible is God's message to man? Yes. Do I believe what the Bible says? Yes. That all have sinned? Yes. That nothing I can do can save me from my sin? Yes. That Jesus already did it for me and that He is the only way to God? Yes. Do I want Christ in my life? Do I want to become a Christian?"[1]

After all those "yes's," there was only one answer. He slid off his bed, knelt down on the hardwood floor, and began to pray. He didn't pray a stock prayer; he simply told God what was on his mind: "God, I don't know everything about You. I don't think I ever will. But I know I'm a sinner and I know I want to be forgiven. I know I want Christ in my life, and I want to go to heaven. I want to become a Christian. With that, I accept You. Amen.[2]

Nothing dramatic happened. He climbed back on his bed and kept reading. Deep down, though, he was deeply relieved. He'd made the decision, and ever since then he has walked with Christ. He began getting involved in church and Bible studies, and checked everything he heard against what he read in the Bible. It was not long afterwards that he met his future wife and was on his way to double-A ball.

In 1980 and 1981, Orel played for the San Antonio Dodgers. He did not have his best seasons. He went 5–9 in 1980 with a 3.55 ERA and 7–6 in 1981 with a 4.68 ERA. But he was learning the moves, attitudes, regimen, and system that every big-league pitcher must learn sooner or later. You can't go on guts and luck in the major leagues; there has to be discipline and use of your head. Orel set out to become a "thinking man's pitcher." He knew he didn't have the strength of a Dwight Gooden or Roger Clemens to "blow people away" with his fastball, so he had to learn the technique that went into a potent curve, a solid slider, and a popping fastball. He worked hard and moved up to triple A in 1982.

Orel had two strong seasons at Albuquerque, going 9–6 and 10–8, respectively. His ERA was still in the high threes and low fours, but he was improving. He won the Mulvey Award as the top rookie in Dodger spring training. Still, he was sent back to Albuquerque, where he kept on throwing the hard ones. He ended up pitching eight innings in the big leagues with Los Angeles in 1983, but had a 0–0 record.

In 1984, Orel made the Dodgers and began pitching relief. But it wasn't until Tommy Lasorda himself preached to Orel a personal "Sermon on the Mound" that Orel got it together. Orel was being too careful, and he was getting clobbered. Lasorda encouraged him. "Who do you think these hitters are, Babe Ruth?" he said to Orel. "Ruth's dead! You've got good stuff. If you didn't, I wouldn't have brought you up. Quit bein' so careful! Go after the hitter! Get ahead in the count! Don't be so fine with him and then find yourself forced to lay one in! If I had your stuff, I'd 'a' been in the Hall of Fame!"[3]

Lasorda's talk fired Orel up. When a tight relief spot came up two days later, Orel volunteered. As he strode out to the mound, Lasorda hollered out the nickname he'd given Orel two days before, "C'mon, Bulldog! You can do it, Bulldog! You're my man, Bulldog!" Orel pitched three innings and gave up only one run. He felt as if he was on a ten-mile high. He had made it to the majors, and he had done it!

On May 26, 1984, Orel started his first game. He joined the starting rotation a month later. With that first start began the longest consecutive-scoreless-innings streak of the year—thirty-three and two-thirds innings without allowing a run. He threw four shutouts in a row and won the Pitcher of the Month award. He came in third in Rookie of the Year voting and went 11–8 with a 2.66 ERA.

The next year, 1985, Orel pitched even better. He logged a 19–3 record, had the best winning percentage in baseball (.864), and won his last eleven decisions. His record still stands for a Dodger pitcher. He didn't win the Cy Young Award, but he was third in the voting. After that season, his lawyer negotiated his first million-dollar contract.

The next two seasons didn't go as well. Orel logged a 14–14 record in 1986 with a 3.85 ERA. In 1987, he repeated the effort, finishing 16–16. He wasn't on track.

Then came 1988.

The Dodgers finished fourth in the league both 1986 and 1987. In 1988, Fernando Valenzuela, the Dodgers' ace, suffered from a sore arm most of the season. No one knew who could fill his place. They lost their opener to the Giants. But something was happening: Orel Hershiser started to get hot.

After losing the opener, the Dodgers won five straight games. In April, Orel was Pitcher of the Month with five wins, no losses. His ERA was 1.56.

Then, despite a disappointing May, Orel came back with a 5–1 record in June, with one shutout. By August 14, Orel was 16–7 and was being looked at as Cy Young material. He lost one more game in August against the Mets. Then, on August 30, he started something that is the stuff of fame. After the fifth inning that day, Orel held the Expos scoreless. No one noticed anything different, of course, but that was only the beginning.

Just how easy is it to pitch one, let alone several, scoreless innings?

In a runless streak, there is no distinction between earned and unearned runs, as there is in ERA calculations. It doesn't matter how the other team gets a run: a run is a run. All it takes is one hard-swinging slugger to whack your best pitch into the center-field stands and the streak is over. Or one muffed grounder with a man on third and the streak is over. Or a walk, a sacrifice bunt, a grounder to the right side, and a broken-bat single and the streak is over.

Almost every team has several .300-plus hitters. If a team sends up four batters in an inning, or more likely, five, the odds are that they'll get one and two-thirds hits. If one of those men gets to third with one or fewer outs, the odds on scoring are tremendous. A sacrifice fly can bring him home. A suicide squeeze. A dribbler. A bad hop. An error. Or, of course, any earned hit, some of which can be pretty leaky—bloopers, squibs, texas leaguers, broken-bat singles, grounders with eyes.

Scoreless innings are hard to come by, especially in sequence. That's part of the reason a shutout is an event, and a no-hitter is headline news. A perfect game—three up and three down for nine innings—is cause for nomination to the Hall of Fame.

After the four scoreless innings against Montreal, Orel next shut out the last-place Braves on four hits. Then on September 10, he blanked a hot Cincinnati Reds team that had won eight of their last ten games. The tight spot in that game occurred in the third inning when Orel loaded the bases with two outs. But Eric Davis, who had 25 homers at that point, was called out watching the ball go by. The rest of the game, Orel allowed seven scattered hits, walking three.

It was his second shutout in a row. The streak was still alive, though no one was paying much attention yet. Twenty-two scoreless innings. More importantly, Orel had won his twentieth game, the first time in his major league career.

September 14 came with the Dodgers at home against Atlanta. Orel had only had three days' rest but Lasorda put him in.

Orel ran into trouble once, in the seventh inning. A double and an infield error put runners at first and third, no outs. Ozzie Virgil grounded to Franklin Stubbs, the first baseman, who held the runner at third and made the putout. Men on second and third, one out. Orel intentionally walked the next batter in order to get to the Braves' pitcher, Rick Mahler, whom he fanned. Two gone, bases still loaded. Top of the order. Ron Gant.

Orel started to pitch a curve, but the moment it left his hand he knew he'd hung it. Gant slammed it into left field. Was it gone? Kirk Gibson had bad legs at the time, but he ran his heart out and grabbed the ball while crashing into the wall. Orel was home free and out of his worst jam so far. And still scoreless after 29 innings.

The game remained 0–0 going into the ninth, but the Dodgers managed to score in the bottom half of the inning and won, 1–0. It was Orel's third shutout in a row. Thirty-one innings without score. People were writing about it now. When asked about whether he could break Don Drysdale's record, Orel said, "I see Don's record as one that won't be broken. I don't see it happening."[4] He was still twenty-seven and two-thirds innings away from breaking

that record. And he only had three starts left in the season. Even with three nine-inning shutouts, he'd be two-thirds of an inning short.

So much for the record.

Or was it?

Orel's second son had been born two days before his next scheduled start, in Houston. But there were complications. Jordan lay in an incubator gasping for air. Orel didn't want to leave home and his newborn, but he felt he was paid to

pitch when his team needed him. And that was now. He flew out of L.A. for Houston the night before the game. Just before he left, though, Jordan was moved from intensive to intermediate care. He felt there was nothing more he could do. The best thing for him and Jordan was for him to pitch his best in Houston.

He ended up pitching one of his best games that night. He allowed only four singles and no walks. The Dodgers won again, 1–0. The streak now stood at 40 scoreless innings. Suddenly, everyone was paying attention. And many were saying the Cy Young Award was in sight for Orel Hershiser. He had won 22 games so far that year, the most for a Dodger since Sandy Koufax won 27 in 1966.

In Orel's next game, something happened that was "déjà vu all over again," as Yogi Berra would say. Drysdale, in the forty-fifth inning of his streak, loaded the bases with no one out and went to a 2–2 count on batter Dick Dietz. Then he hit him with the next pitch. The run scored, and Drysdale's streak was over, right? No! The umpire said Dietz didn't move to get out of the way of the ball. (If a batter fails to get out of the way and is hit, it isn't a free base, it's a ball.) Now the count was 3–2. Drysdale miraculously got Dietz and the next two hitters out. Drysdale's streak would go thirteen and two-thirds more innings.

The same kind of thing happened to Orel against

the Giants in the third inning, the forty-third of the streak. Jose Uribe led off with a single. Then the Giants' pitcher Atlee Hammaker tried to bunt him to second, and Orel tripped going after the ball: both runners were safe. Brett Butler, up next, grounded to third, where Jeff Hamilton went for the double play at second and first. Uribe was out, but Butler beat the relay and there were now men at first and third, one out. Now almost anything could score a run—a fly into the outfield, a hit, an error, a bad throw, a passed ball. Orel had to press for a double play. He bore down with a sinker to Ernest Riles. Riles grounded to Steve Sax at second, who whipped it to Alfredo Griffin, who threw wide to first. The run scored and the streak was ov—

Wait a minute! What's with the second-base umpire? Brett Butler had run wide of the baseline at Griffin to cause the bad throw. He's out and the runner at first is out too. No run scored. The inning was over. The streak was still on! Tommy Lasorda said to Orel when he stepped back into the dugout, "Drysdale got his break. Now you got yours."[5]

Orel was hot the rest of the game. He allowed only two more hits and it was another shutout. Orel had gone 49 innings without allowing a run. The media went crazy. He'd climbed ahead of Carl Hubbell's 1933 mark of 45⅓ consecutive innings and Bob Gibson's 47 of 1968. Only Walter Johnson and

Drysdale were ahead of him. Orel had one more start for the year.

But there was a problem. Even if he did pitch one more shutout, he would be two-thirds of an inning short of Drysdale's record. To be sure, the streak would continue on into the next season, but a lot could happen after six months' rest and time off.

Actually, Orel only wanted to tie Drysdale's record, if he did anything. He felt he wasn't even in the same class as Drysdale. The record didn't deserve to be broken.

But as things stood, he couldn't even tie the record.

Perhaps he didn't consider that there was one Eternal Fan in heaven who was also watching!

On September 26 the Dodgers clinched the pennant in the Western Division. They'd be going to the National League Championship Series against the Mets.

On September 28, Orel went up against the Padres. He was 7–4 lifetime against the Padres and had won his last outing against them, 12–2. But the Padres had a lone powerhouse named Tony Gwynn, who had won two National League batting championships and was on his way that year to a third. He could be awesome. Orel knew he'd have to have his "game face" on when going up against him, as well as against the rest of the Padres.

Orel started off with butterflies, but soon was in

the groove. By the sixth inning he'd thrown 65 pitches, 45 of them strikes. Two hits. No walks. He was on, and the game was scoreless.

The last out in the seventh crushed Walter Johnson's record of fifty-five and two-thirds scoreless innings. The Padres home crowd gave Orel a standing ovation. They were now on their feet. Cheering after every out. Silence on every pitch, then the blast of emotion and cheering after.

In the eighth, Roberto Alomar singled. Alomar was always a base-stealing threat, so with two outs, Orel kept throwing to first until he caught Roberto leaning the wrong way. He picked him off. End of inning. Fifty-seven scoreless innings. The crowd was wild.

The top of the ninth came up with the Dodgers also still scoreless. Orel walked out to the mound. By now, though, it was easy. Three ground outs. The game stood at 0–0. Orel had pitched 58 scoreless innings. Miraculously, he had his chance to break Drysdale's record. Nothing but a scoreless extra-inning game could have allowed it. No one had even *thought* of a scoreless extra-inning game, but now it was happening. Maybe God himself was indeed watching!

The Dodgers came up in the top of the tenth. Still no fire. No score. Padres up.

Orel struck out Marvell Wynne to lead it off. But the third strike was wild and got away from the catcher. Wynne made it to first on the passed ball. Runner at first, three outs to go.

Benito Santiago, up next, bunted a sacrifice to put Wynne at second, and to put Orel in trouble. The next batter grounded to short. The throw to first put him out, but Wynne went to third. Garry Templeton stood at the plate. After a conference, everyone decided it would be wise to walk Templeton, to set up a force at second. The runner would stay at third, so it was the logical thing to do.

Ball one. Ball two. Orel started walking back to the mound. Suddenly the catcher threw. Orel had to lunge to spear the ball! It almost ended up in center field, which would have certainly scored the run. Orel smiled wryly at Wynne on third, and Wynne smiled back. It would have been a sorry way to break the streak.

The pitcher, Andy Hawkins, was due up next. He had pitched a shutout so far, as had Orel. But the Padres pulled him and sent in pinch hitter Keith Moreland. Orel got two strikes on him, and then he fouled one off. The next pitch was a high fastball. Moreland went after it. He coughed up a shallow fly ball to right field that Jose Gonzalez pulled in. The inning was over. Ten scoreless innings for a sixth shutout. (However, the game would be a no-decision for Orel because the Dodgers also hadn't scored.)

There it was: 59 consecutive scoreless innings. Five straight shutouts and one ten-inning nondecision. A feat that will stand undoubtedly for years to come. Orel Hershiser had done it. Drysdale's record was gone!

Orel couldn't stop grinning. The Dodgers mobbed him on the mound. Afterwards Orel went in to ice his arm. In his 59-inning streak he had allowed 30 hits, struck out 33, and walked 8. It was a moment for the ages.

Orel would go on to claim the MVP Award in the National League Championship Series against the Mets. He would pitch four times—three starts and one relief appearance—and notch one win and a 1.46 ERA. His first eight innings in the playoffs were scoreless too.

Then, in the World Series against the Oakland Athletics, he would go 2–0 with a 1.00 ERA. He pitched two complete games, a rarity nowadays. The first game was a shutout, and in the second Oakland only scored two runs. In the end, from the beginning of the streak, Orel pitched 101⅔ innings, 96 of them scoreless. He compiled an ERA of 0.62.

For the 1988 season, Orel went 23–8 with an ERA of 2.26. He won his last eleven starts, a Dodger record that still stands. The National League Cy Young Award was his, virtually unanimously. *The Sporting News* named him Major League Player of the Year. *Sports Illustrated* gave him the Sportsman of the Year honor. And the Associated Press voted him Professional Athlete of the Year.

Orel Hershiser had left his mark on history. And who knows, maybe he'll beat it again next year!

Sometimes people ask Orel how he stands the pressure of pitching in front of 50,000 fans and even more through TV. He explains it this way:

It's easy when you know in your heart that a baseball game doesn't mean that much. Yes, it means a lot, and you are supposed to do your best. And yes, you have a responsibility to use your talent. So do the best you can. But then forget about it!

After pitching a bad game, I would lie awake and replay every pitch and criticize myself unmercifully. Now I replay pitches, pull out the positive things, and use them to do better the next time.

If you think you have talent to play baseball, never give up. I was never thought of as a pro prospect because I was considered to be too small. But I knew I had a good arm and always figured I would play in the big leagues one day.[6]

Through it all, Orel maintains a stout and unashamed Christian testimony. He says, "I really believe if you are consistent in your Bible study and prayer life, others are going to recognize what you have and realize it's something they want."[7]

85

One thing very unusual about Orel is that he would be seen singing to himself in the dugout or even on the mound; it was his way of reaching a calm internal peace. The night after the World Series, Orel made an appearance on *Late Night with Johnny Carson*. Johnny asked Orel about the singing.

"Do you just hum, or what? Do you sing?" Johnny asked.

"I sing," Orel answered.

The audience was clapping and cheering, and Orel realized what they wanted. He exclaimed, "I'm not gonna sing!"

Johnny said, "Yes you are! Oh, yes you are!"

There was no way he could avoid it. He had to sing. So he said, "Well, the one I can remember singing the most was just a praise hymn."

Suddenly, the audience went dead quiet.

"As I sat on the bench, I would sing:

'Praise God from whom all blessings flow.

Praise Him all creatures here below.

Praise Him above ye heavenly host.

Praise Father, Son, and Holy Ghost.'"[8]

It was a fitting end to an incredible season, a testimony for the ages. Perhaps even God himself cheered!

1. Orel Hershiser with Jerry B. Jenkins, *Out of the Blue* (Brentwood, Tenn.: Wolgemuth and Hyatt, 1989), 76–77.
2. Hershiser, 76–77.
3. Hershiser, 10.
4. Hershiser, 113.
5. Hershiser, 120.
6. Bill Alexson, *Batting a Thousand* (Nashville: Nelson, 1990), 20–21.
7. Alexson, 20–21.
8. Alexson, 208.